JAPAN

Coloring Book for Grown-Ups

ColoringArtist.com

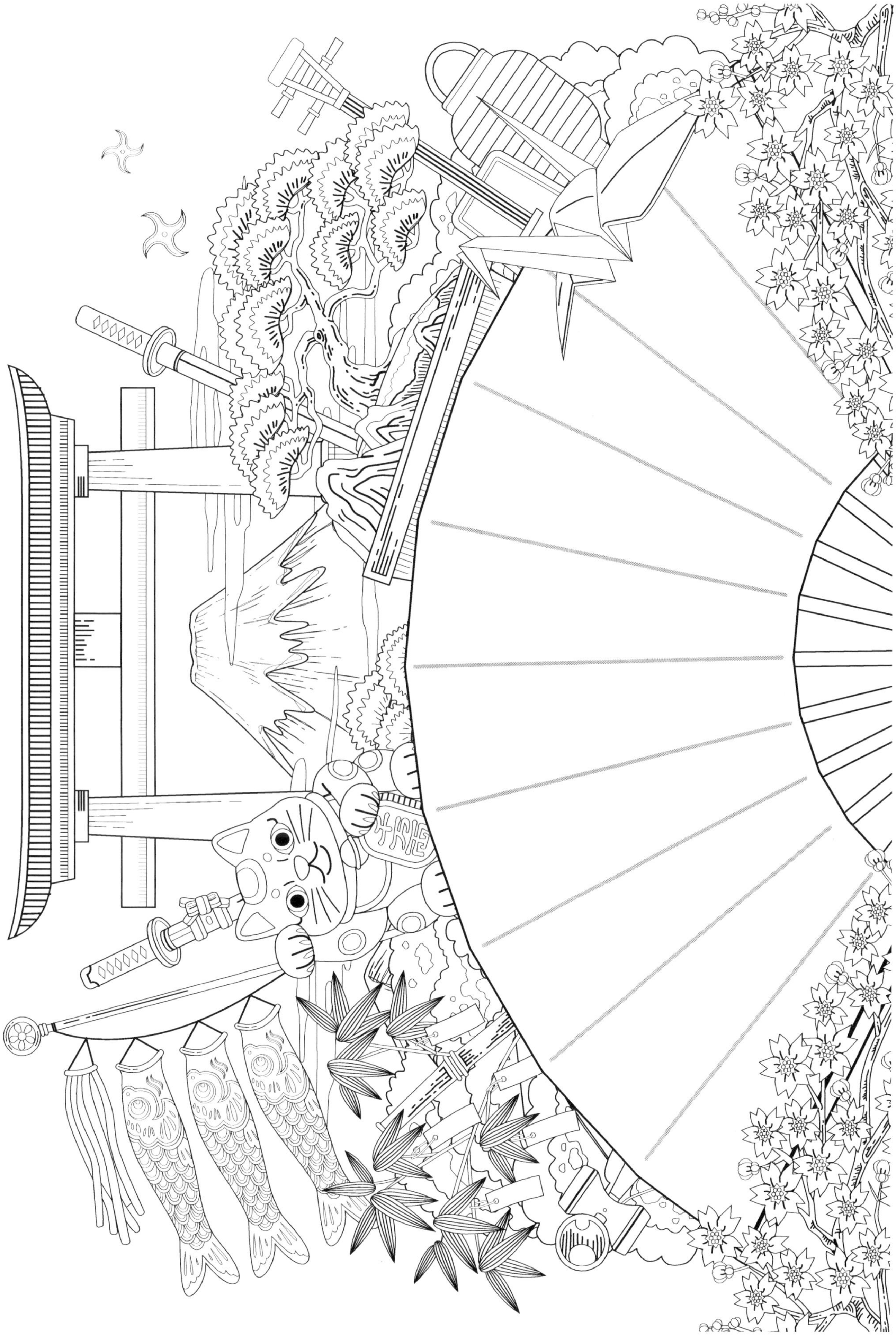

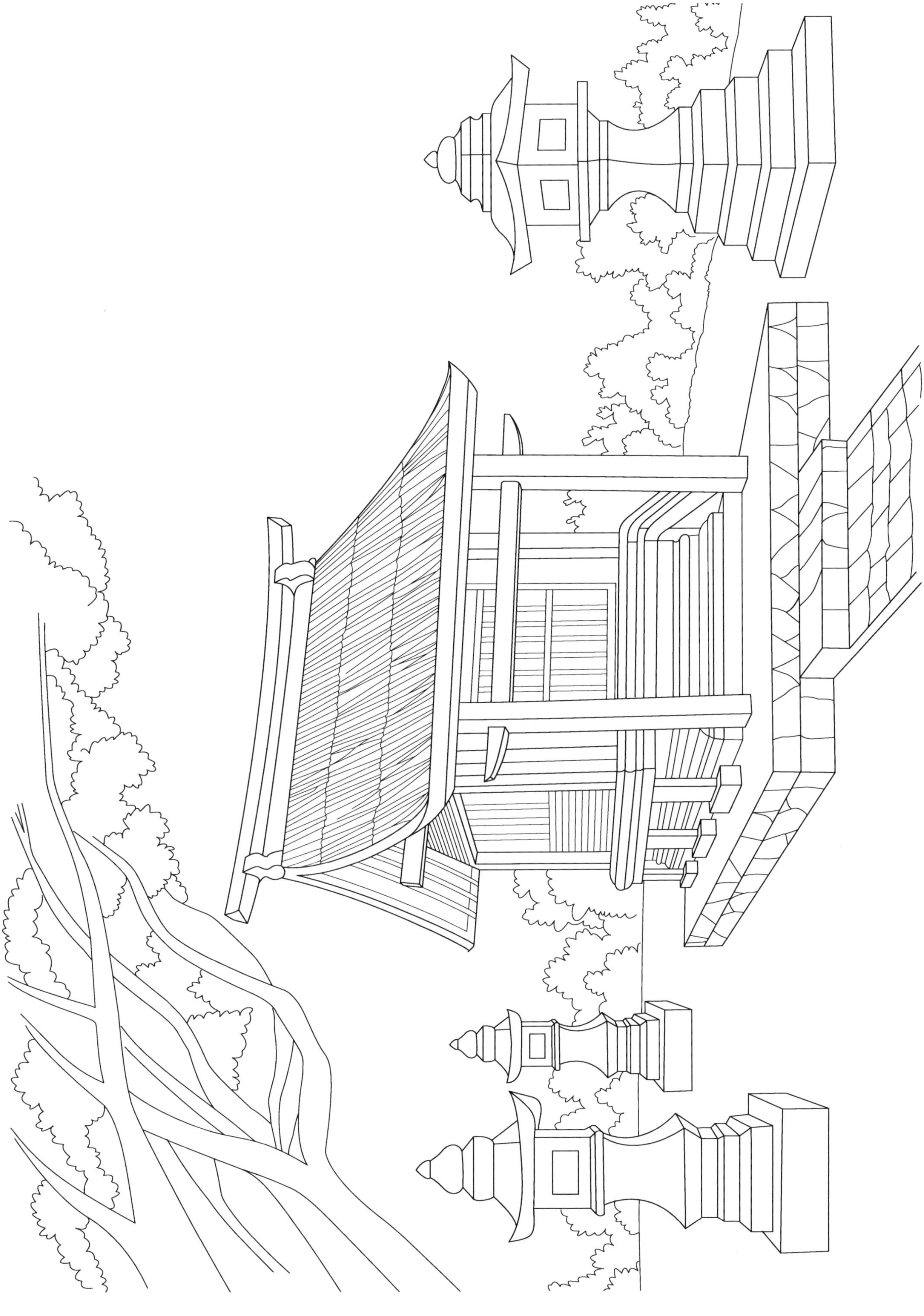

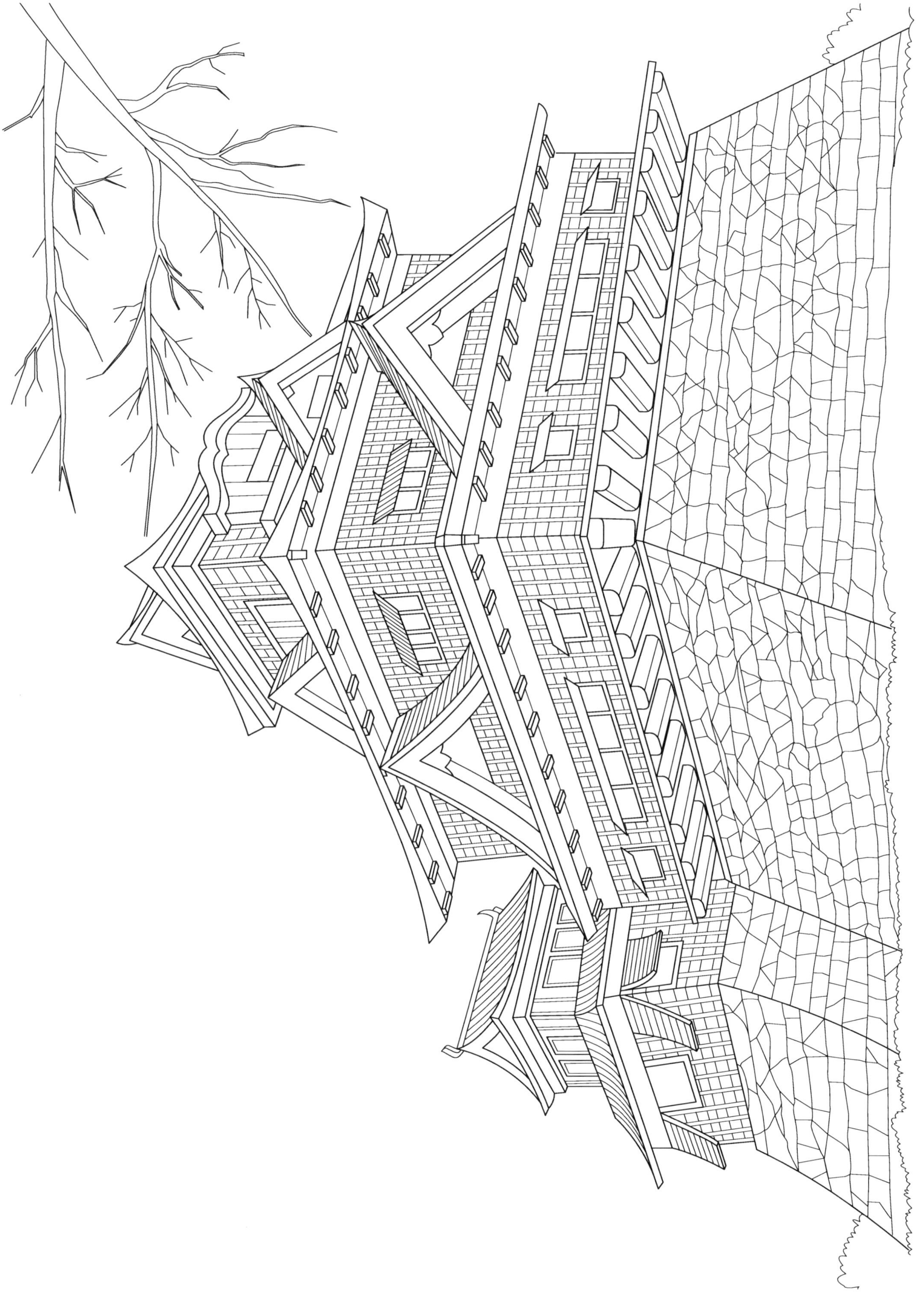

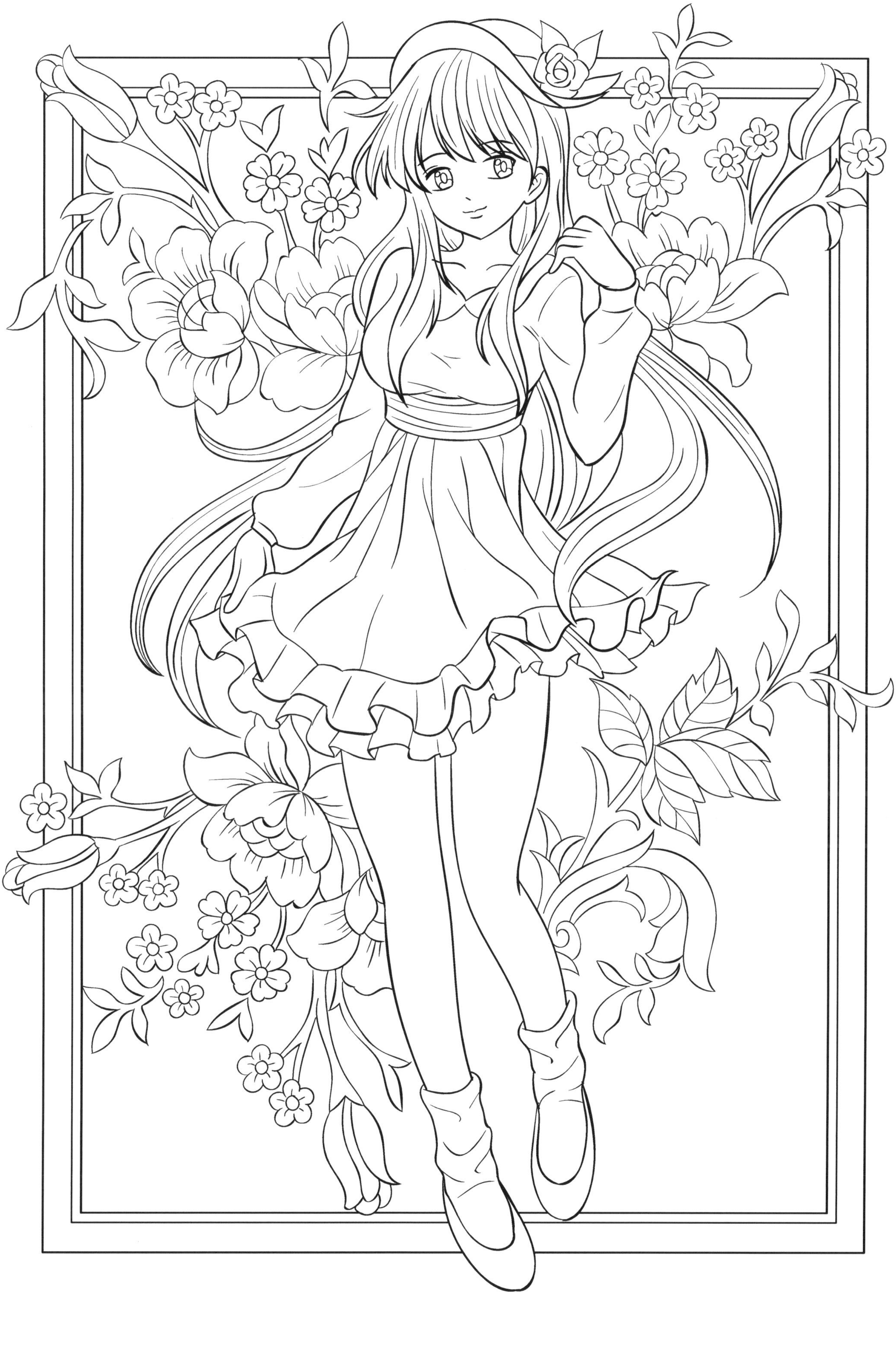

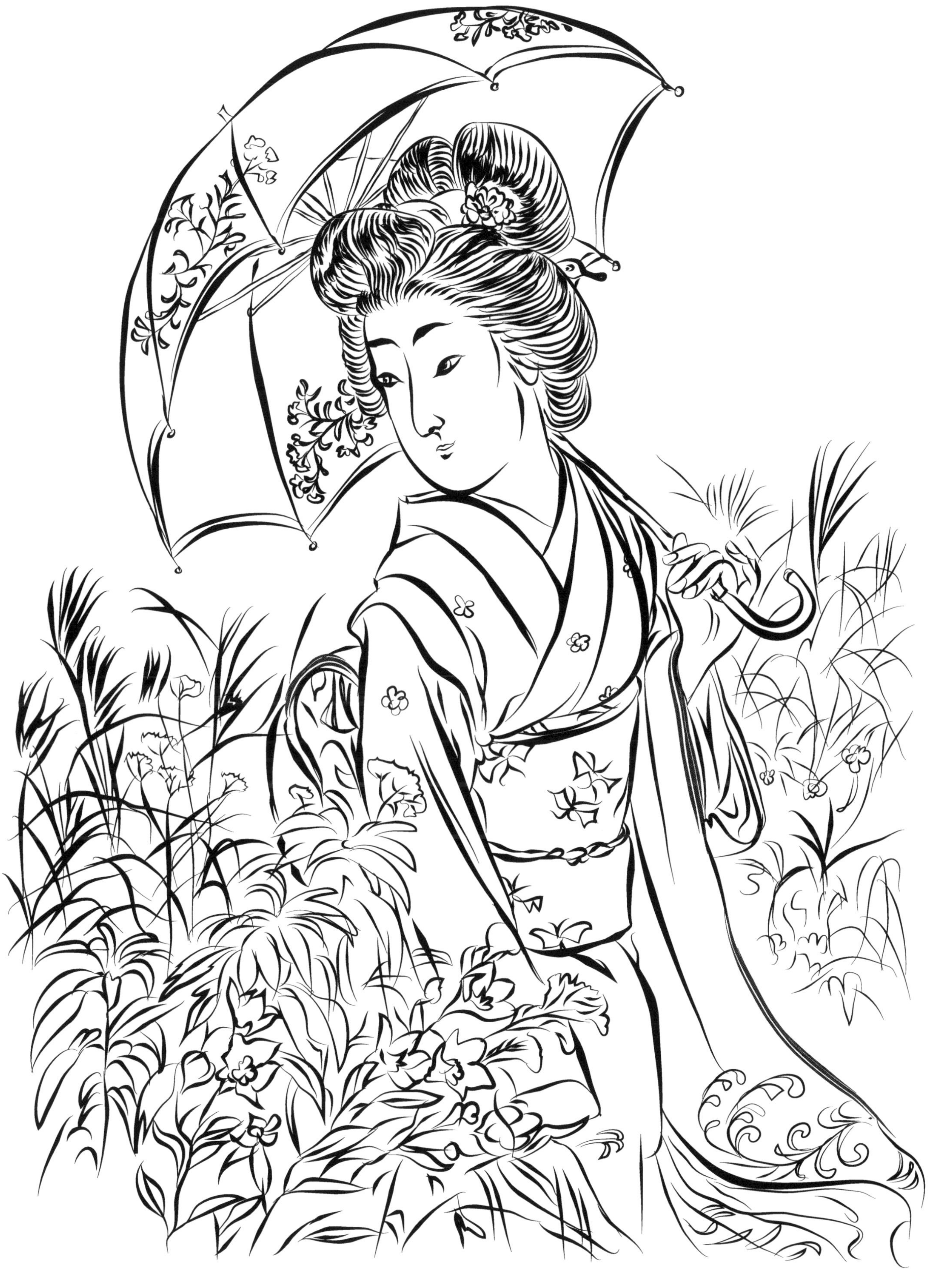

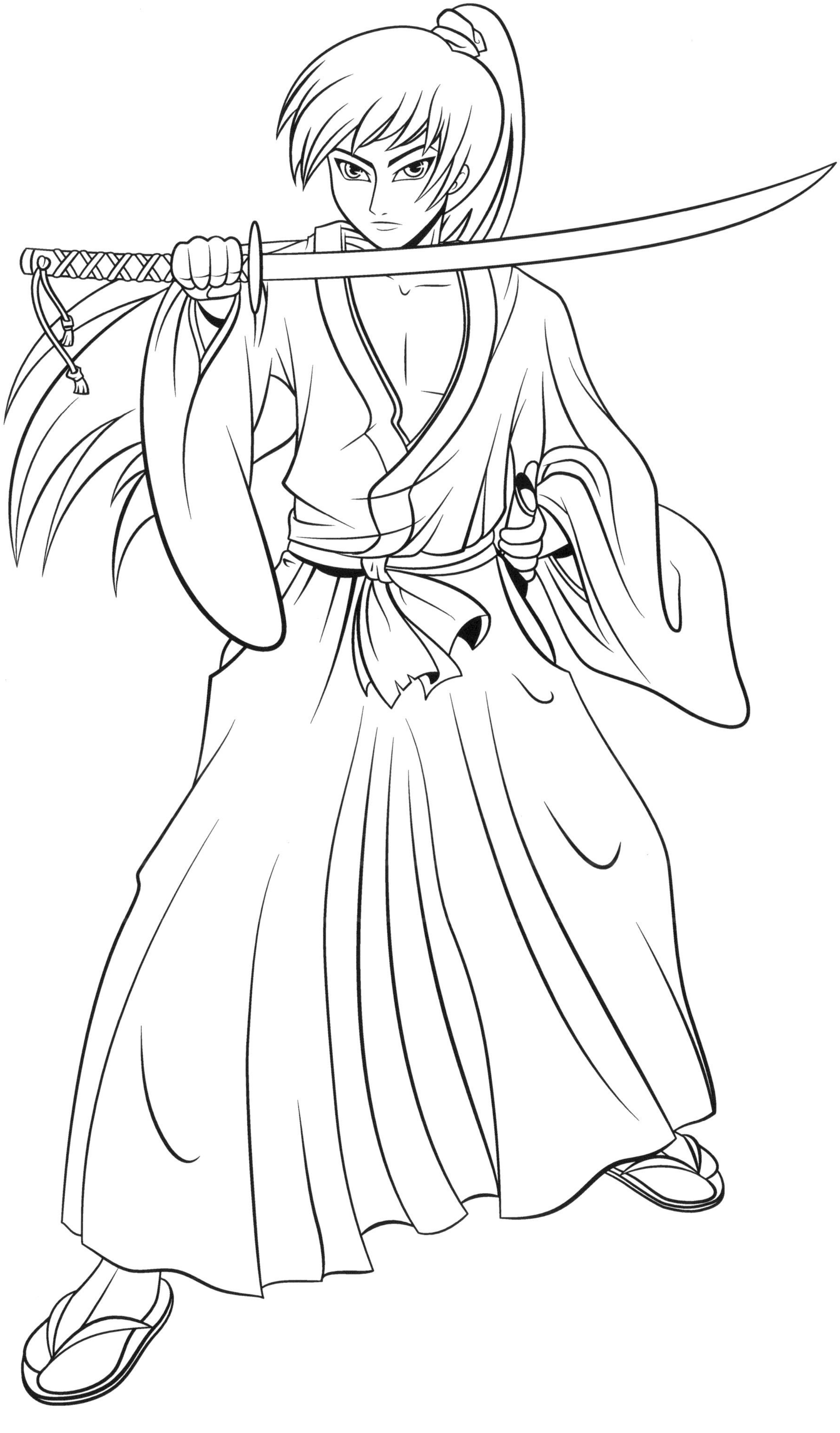

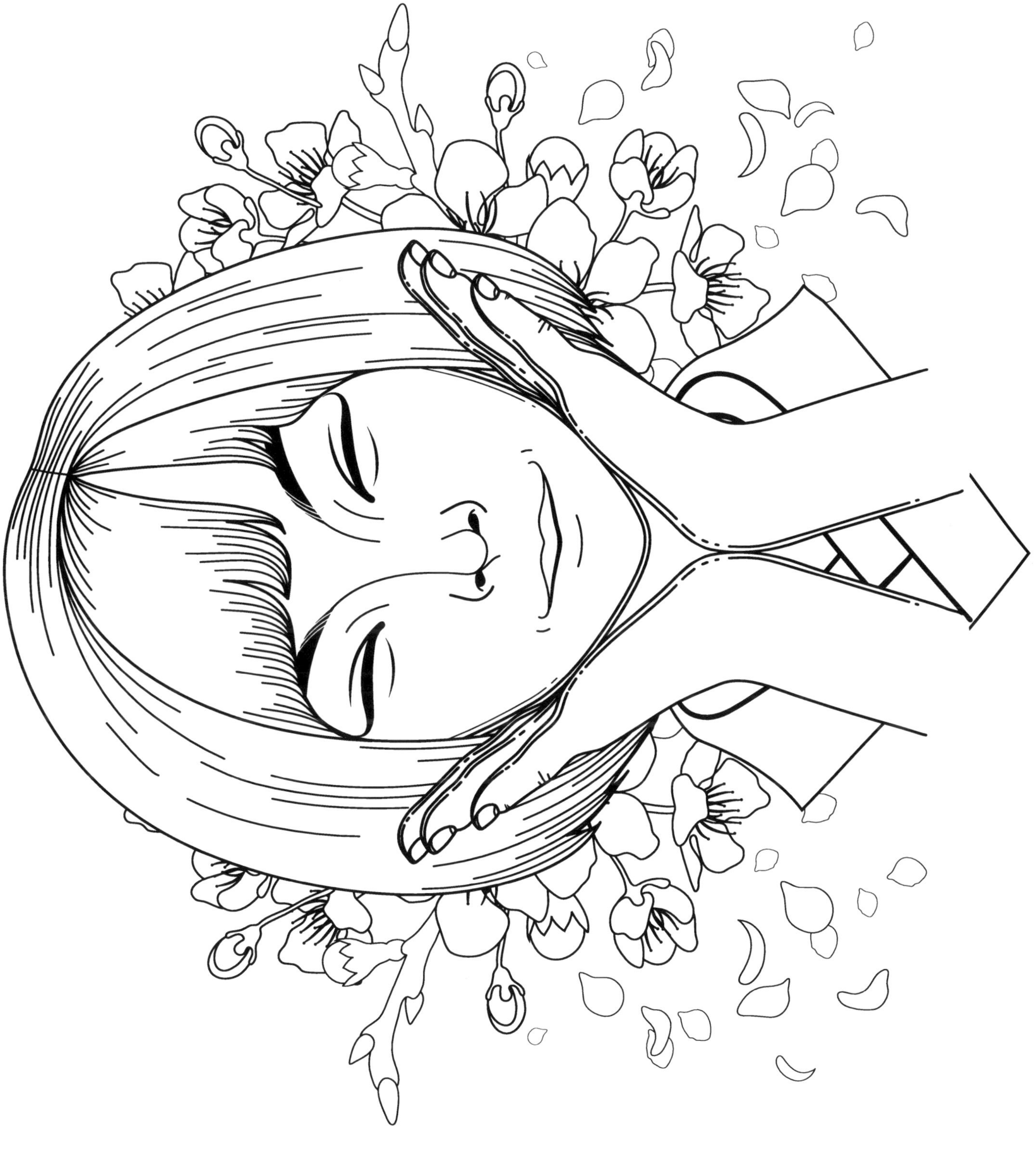

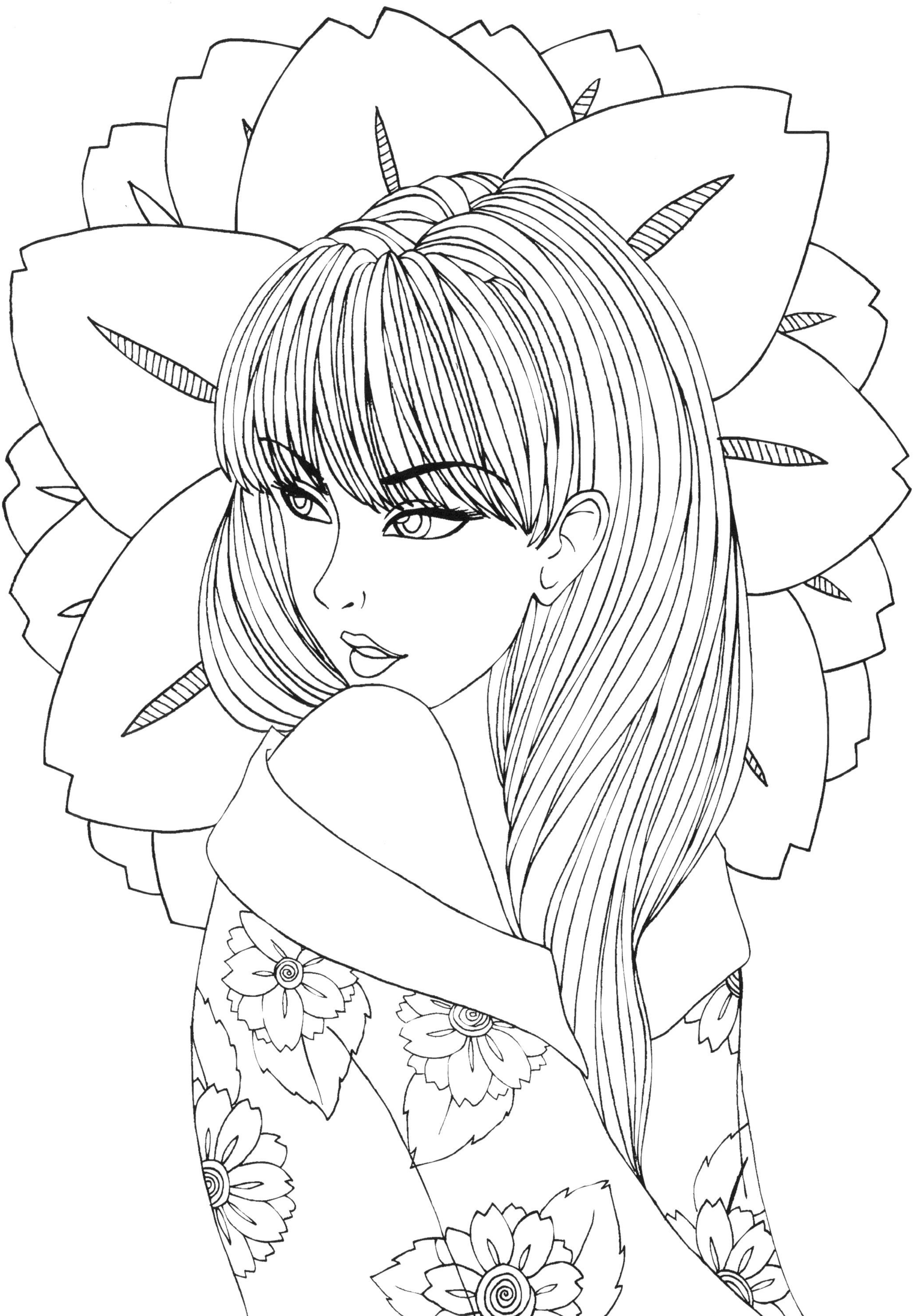

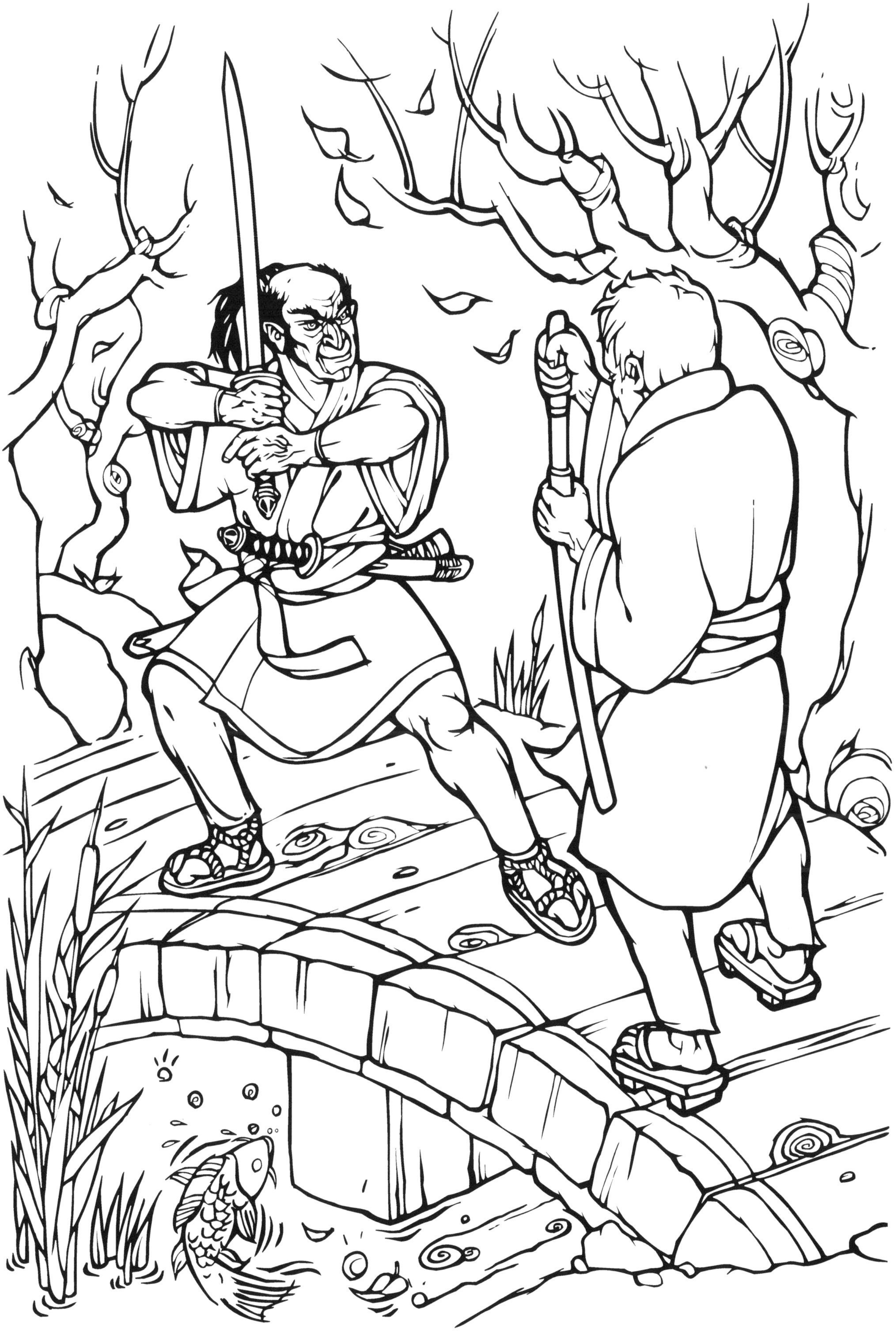

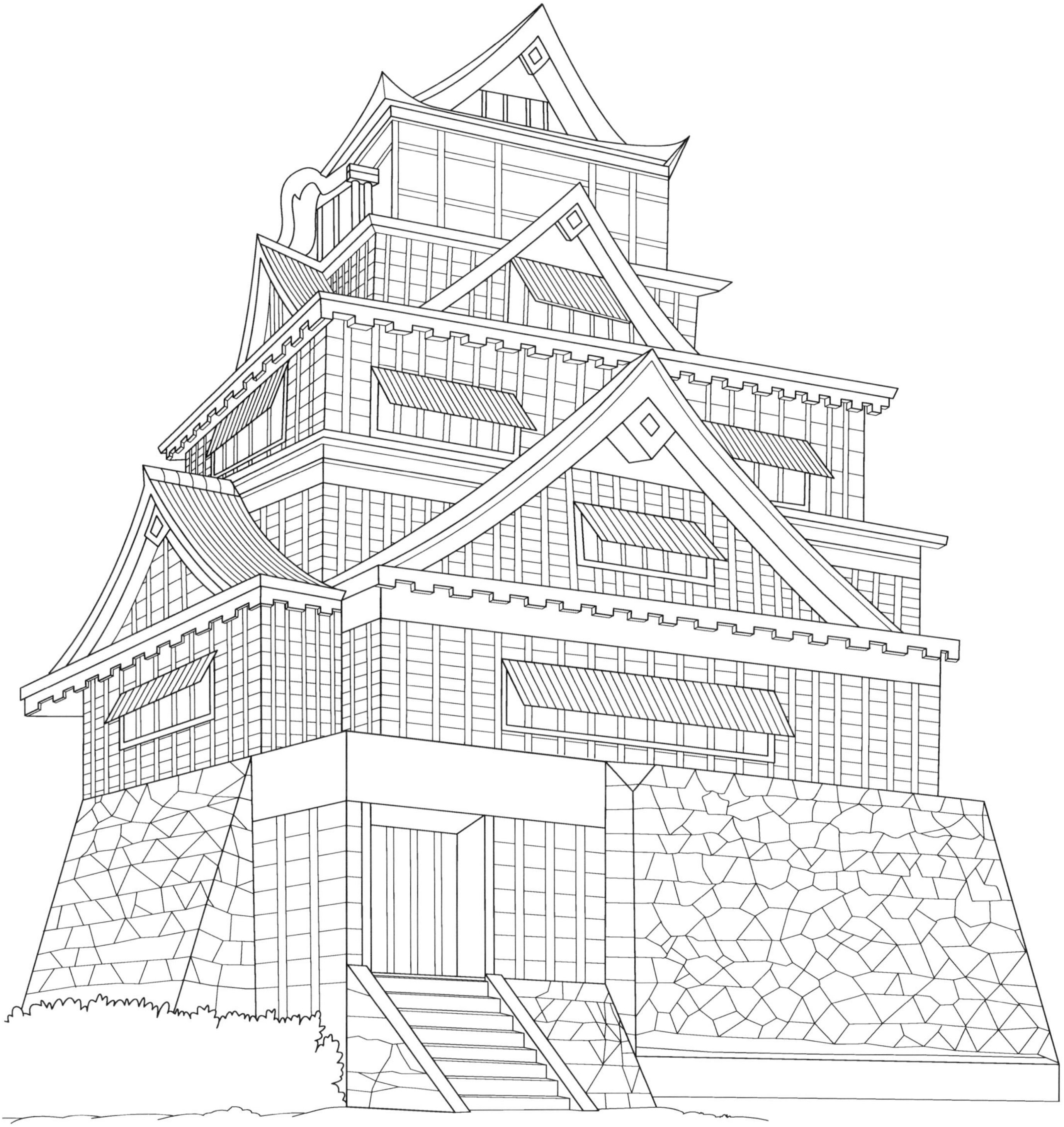

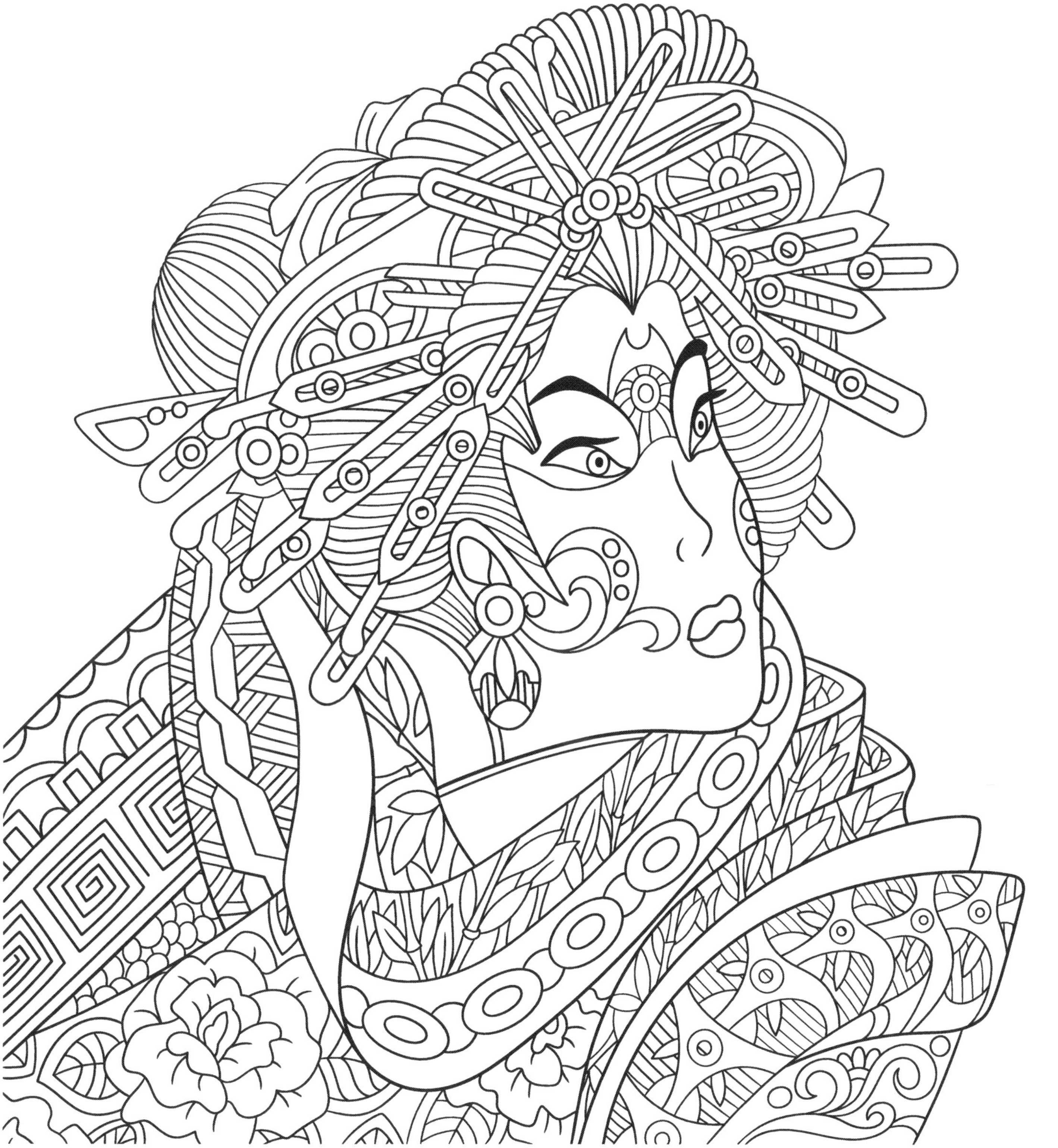

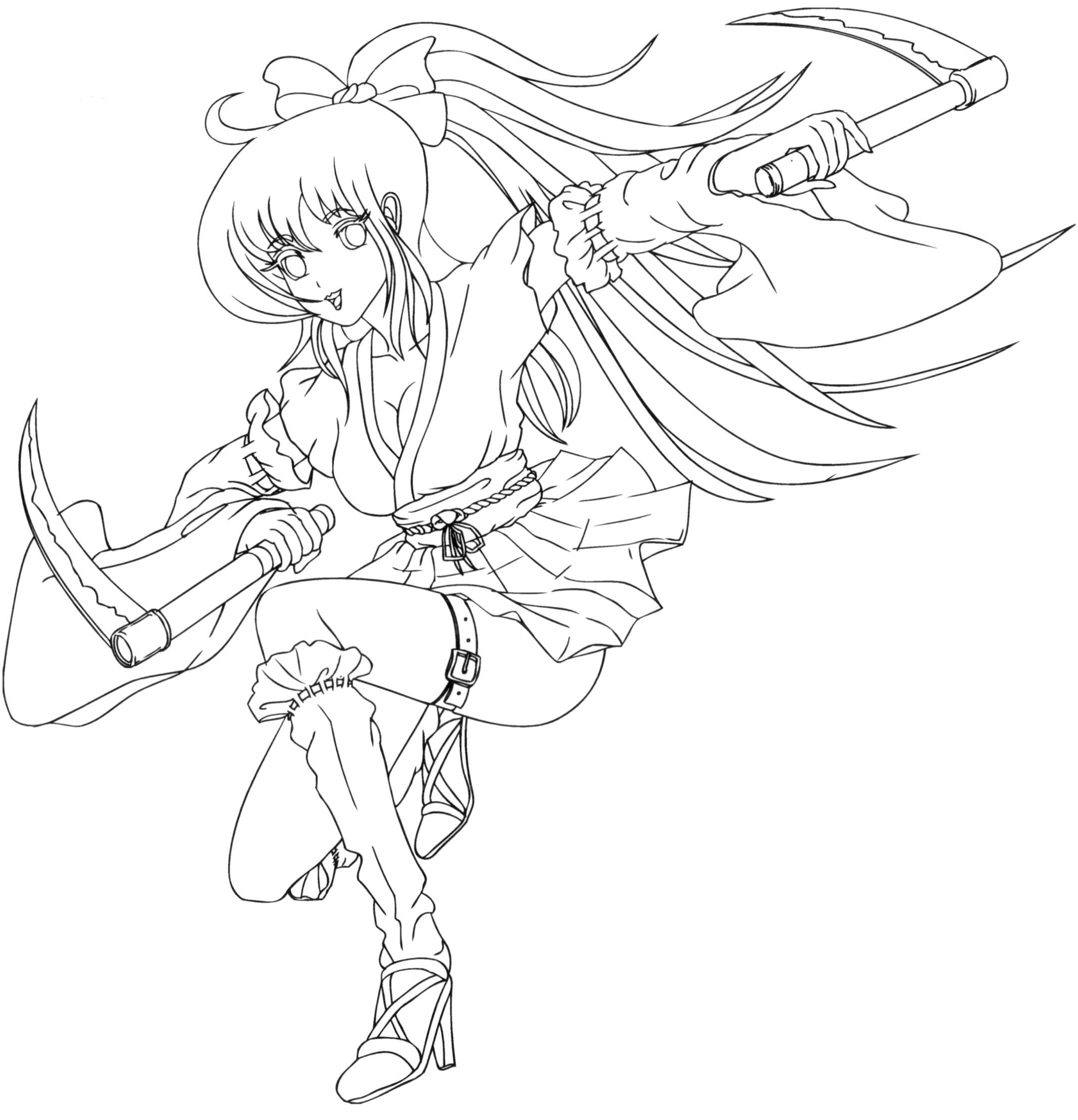

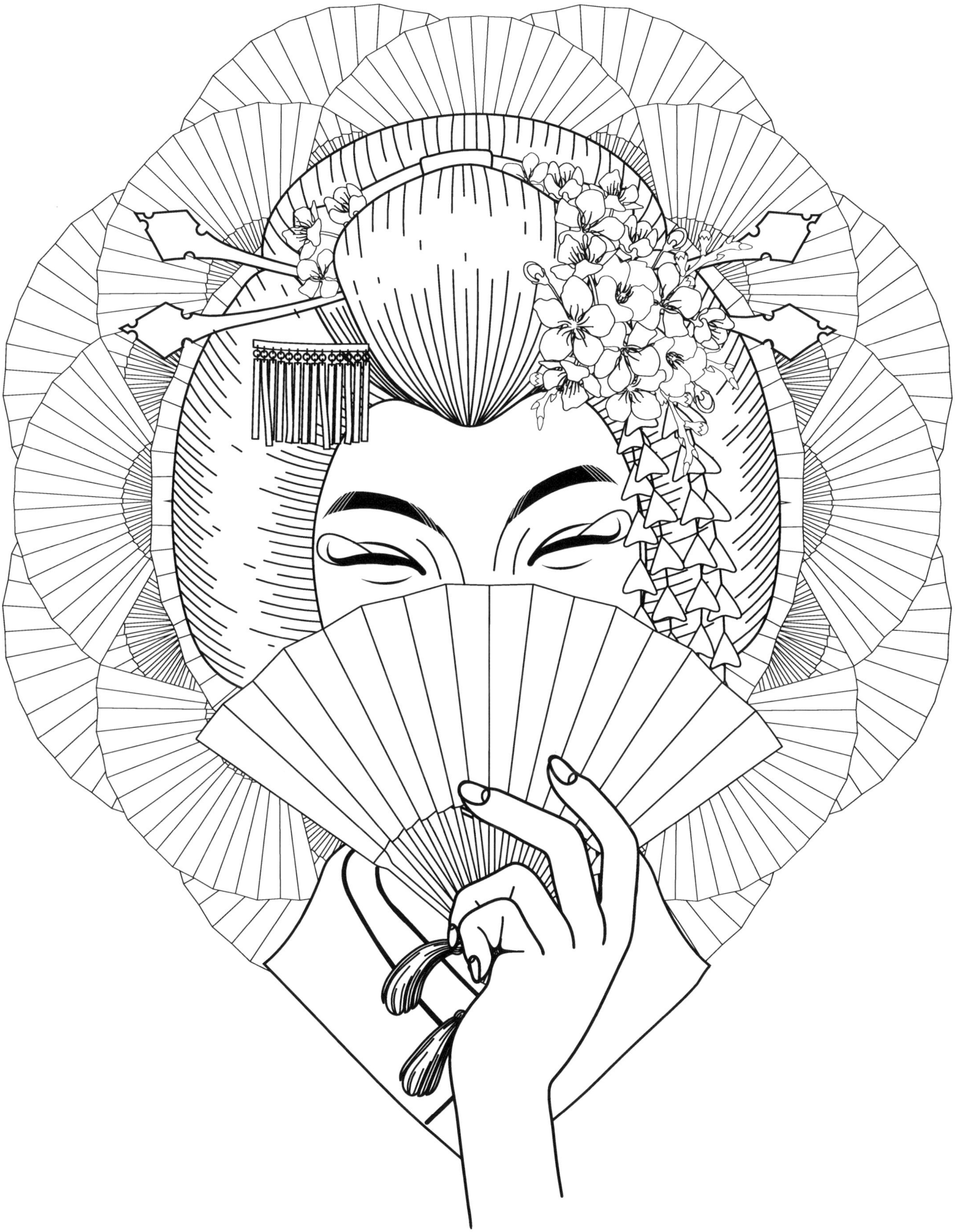

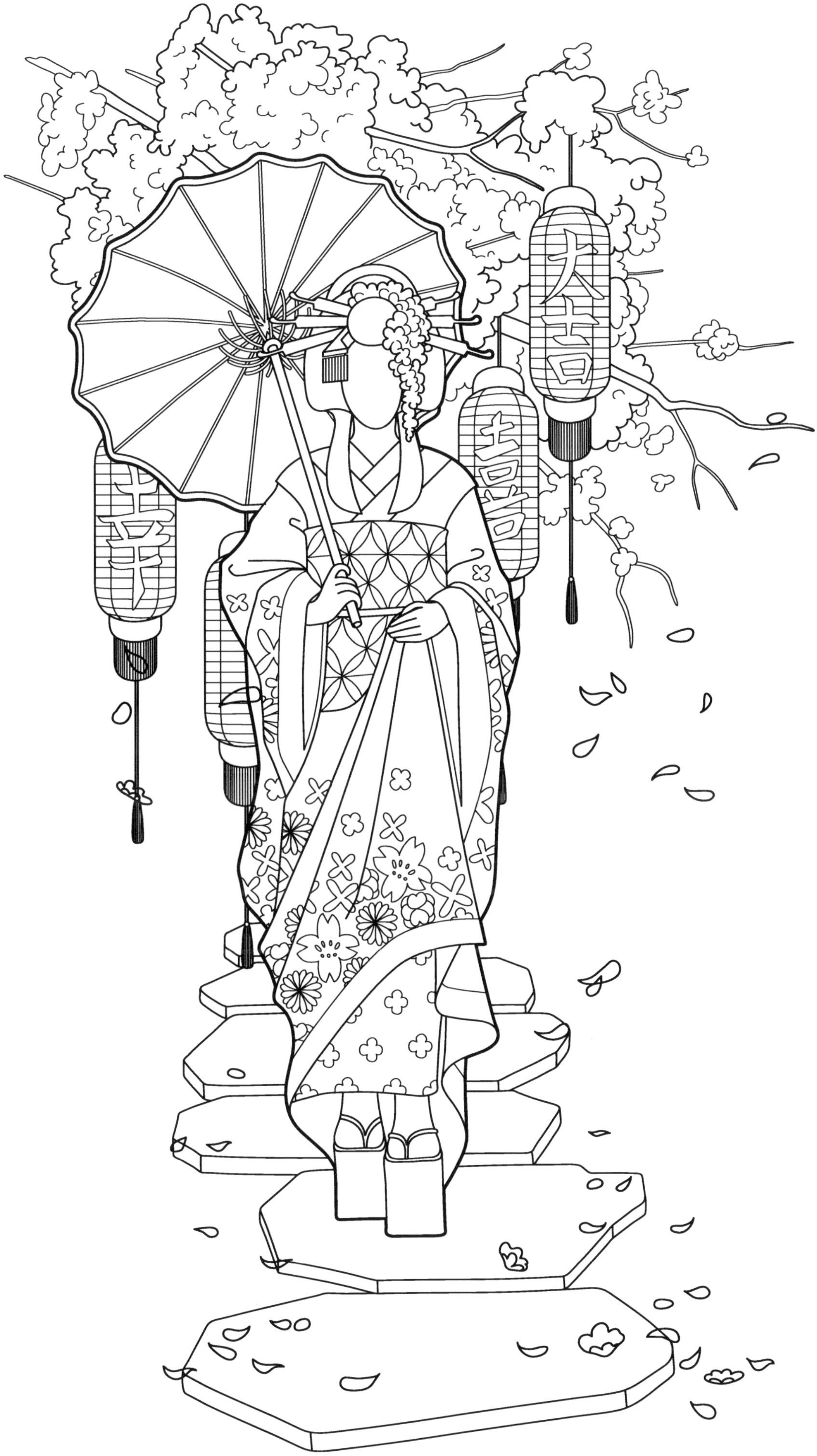
大吉
幸

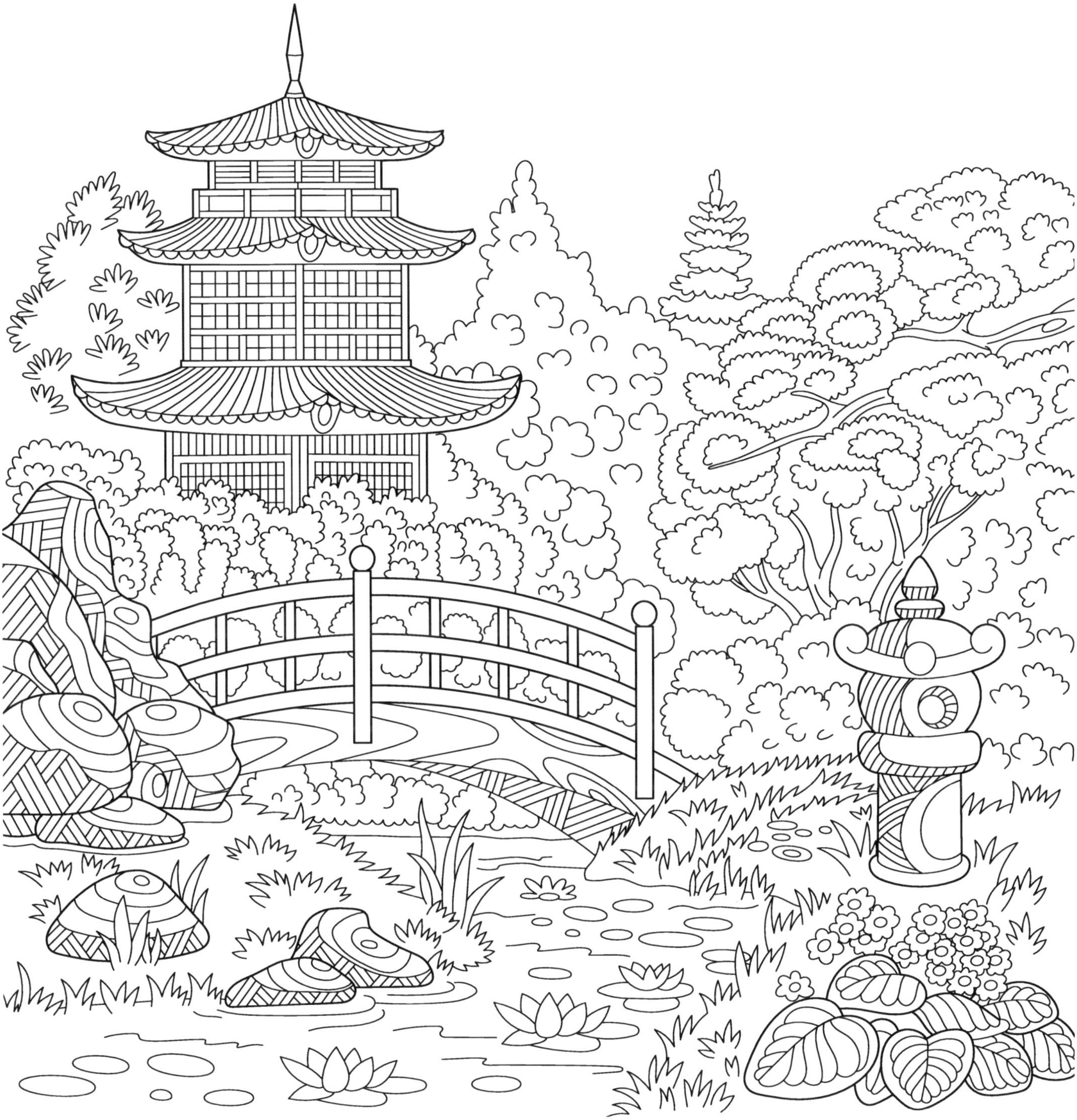

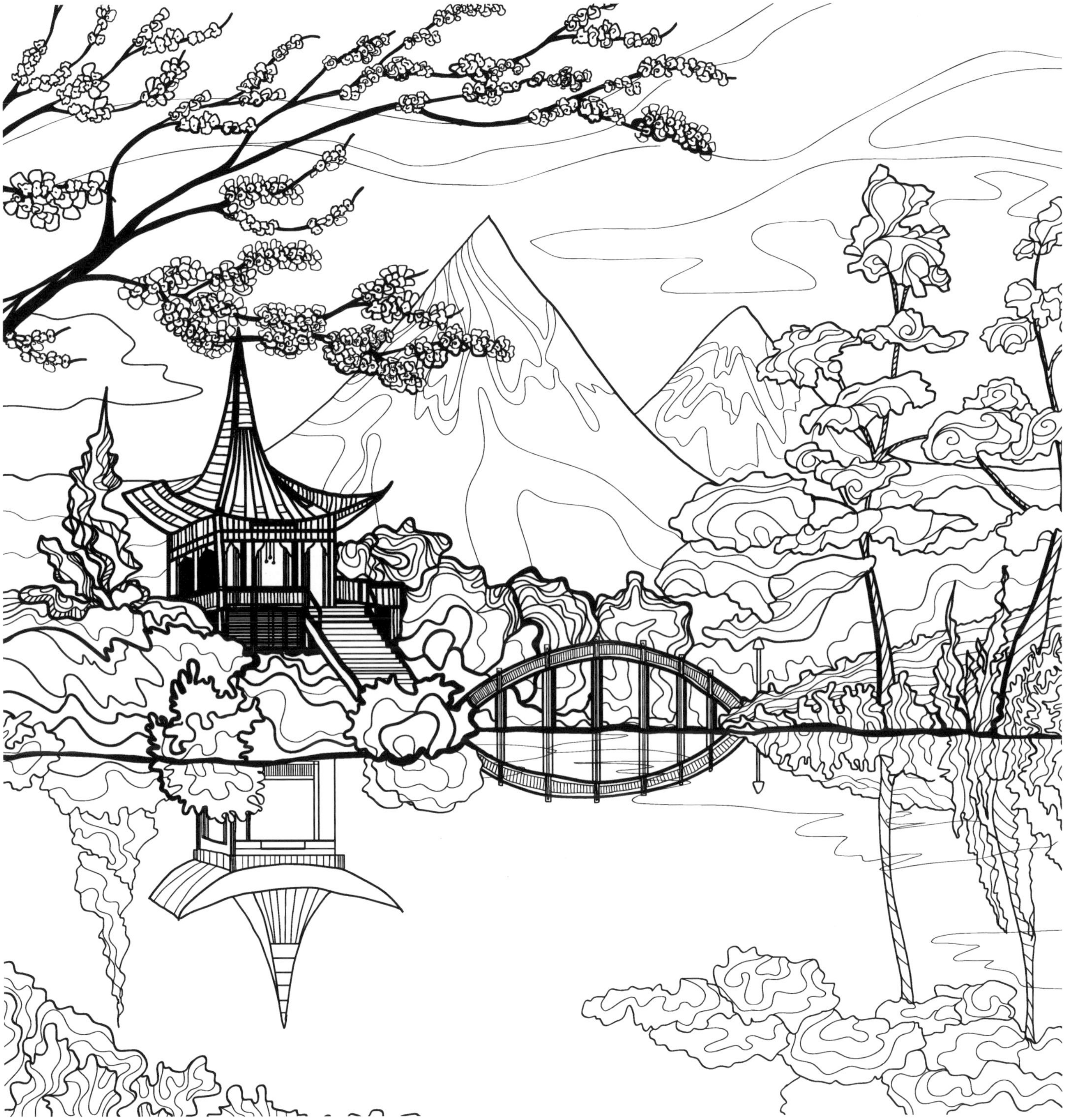

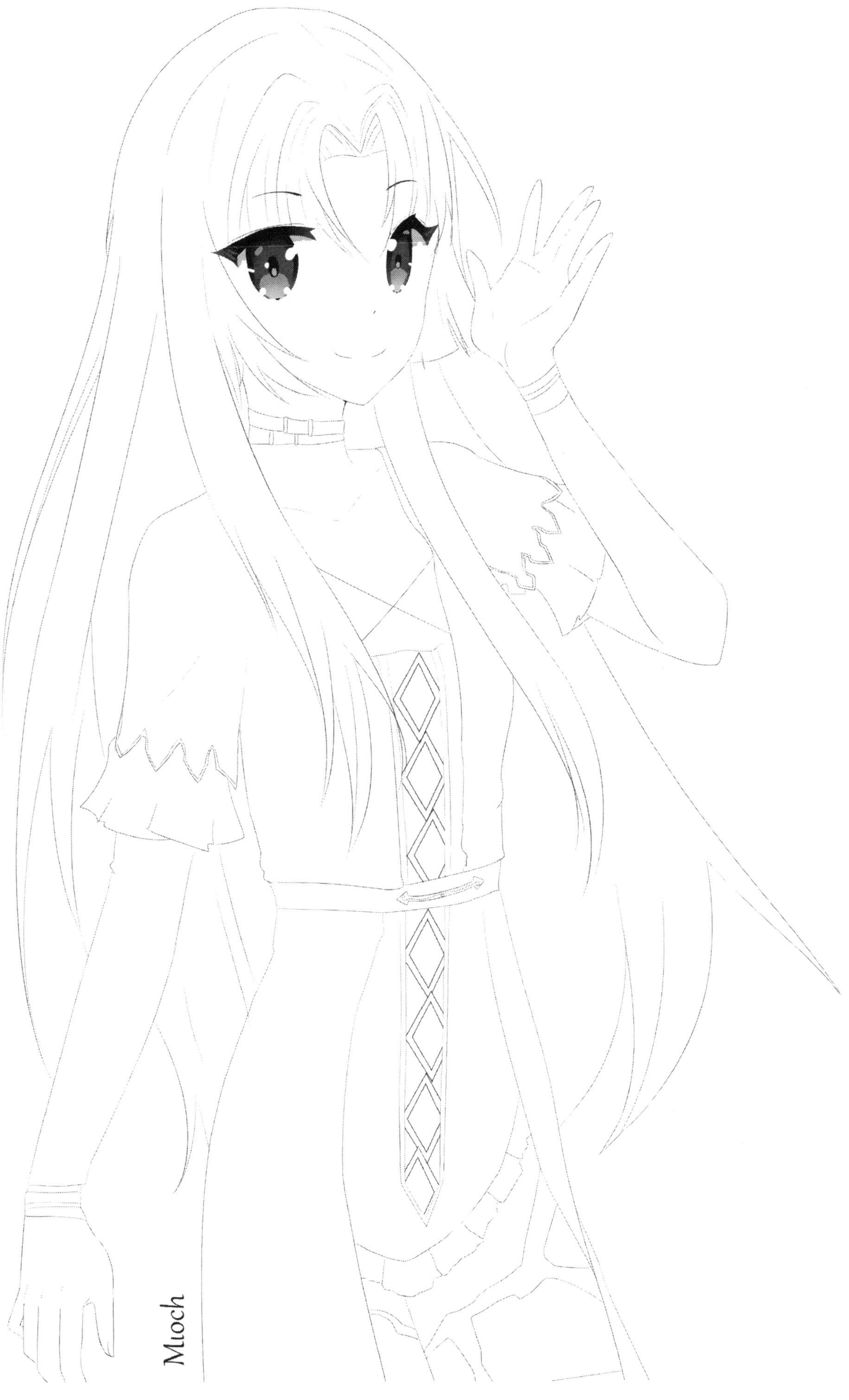
Mioch

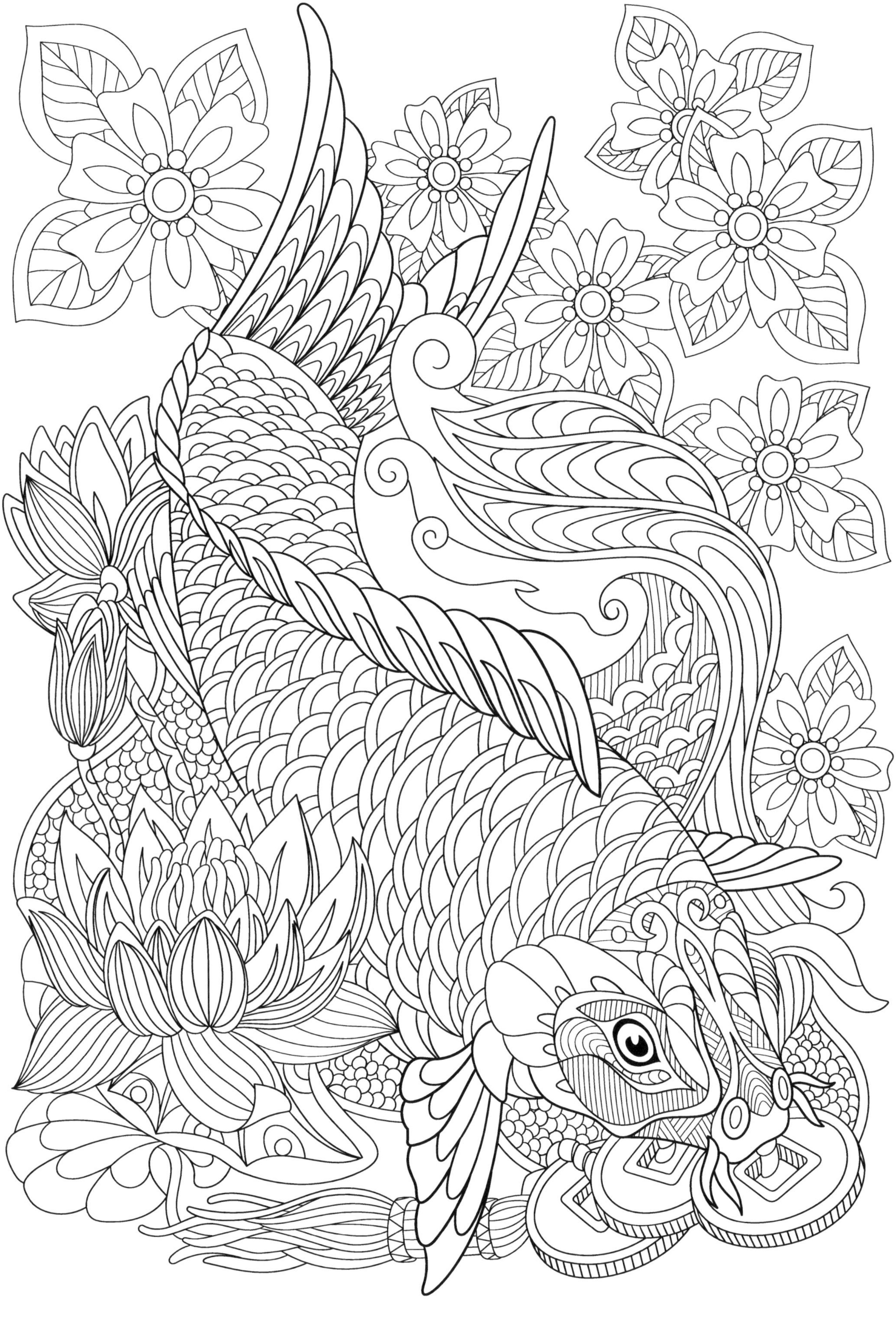

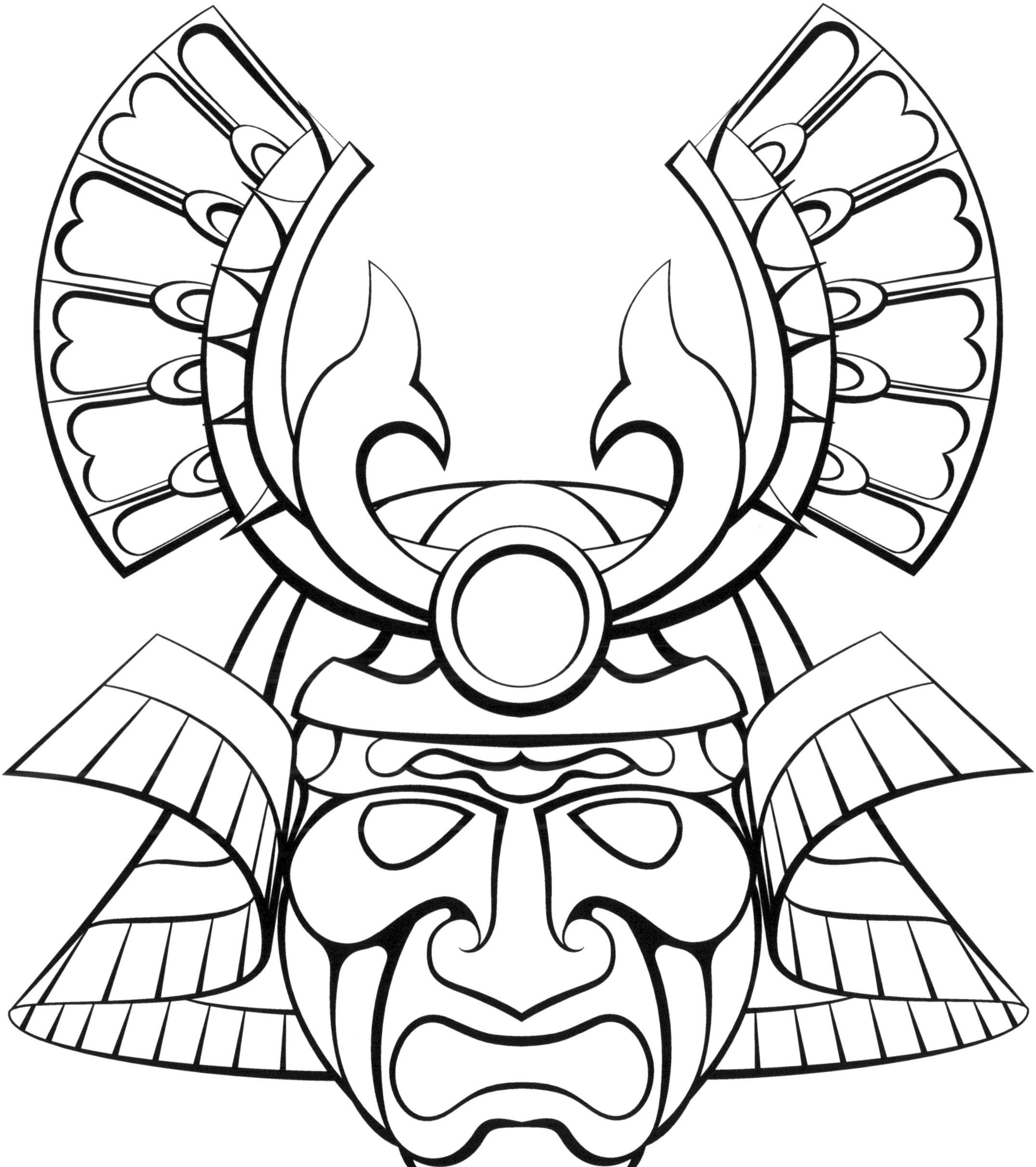

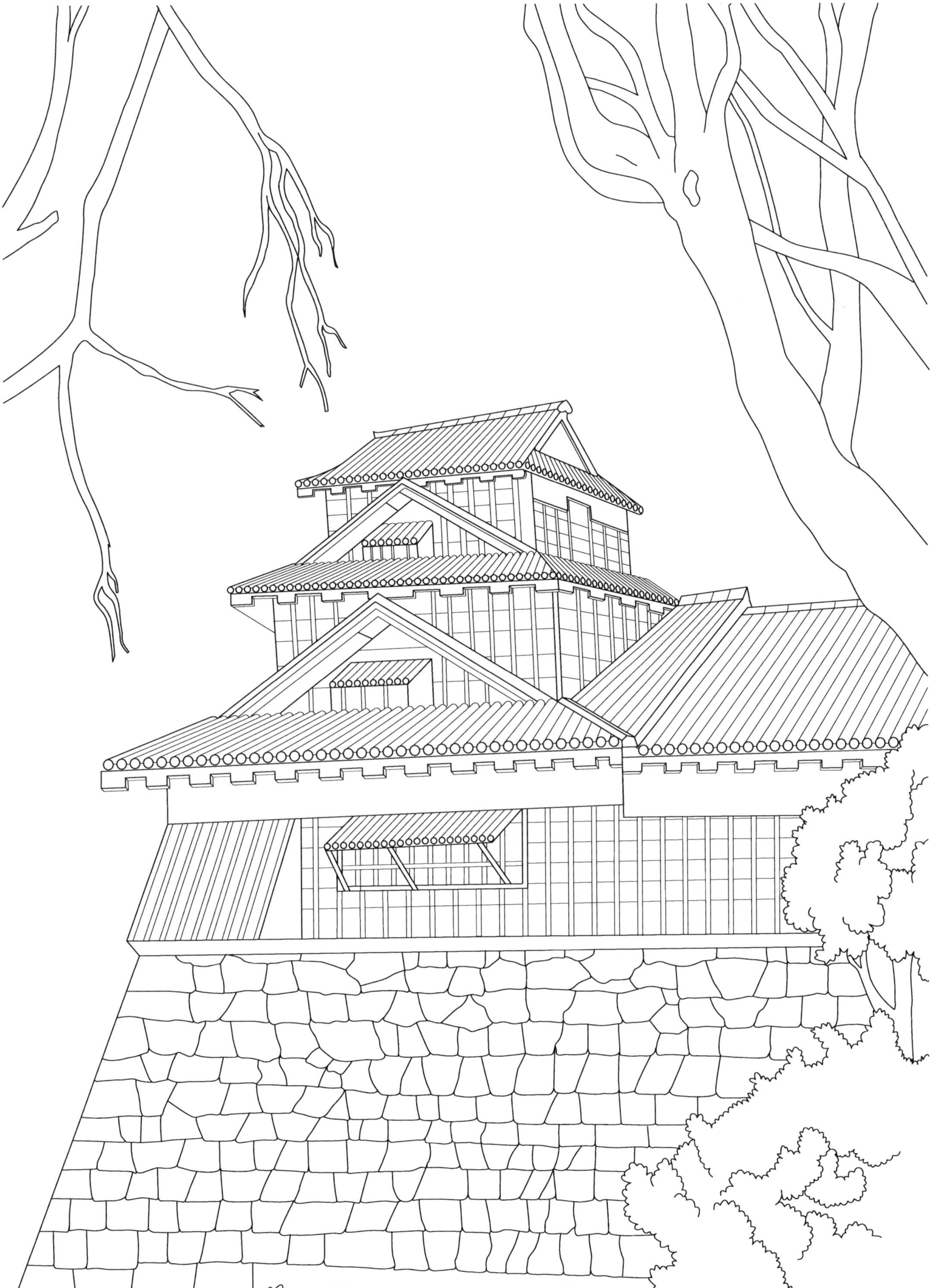

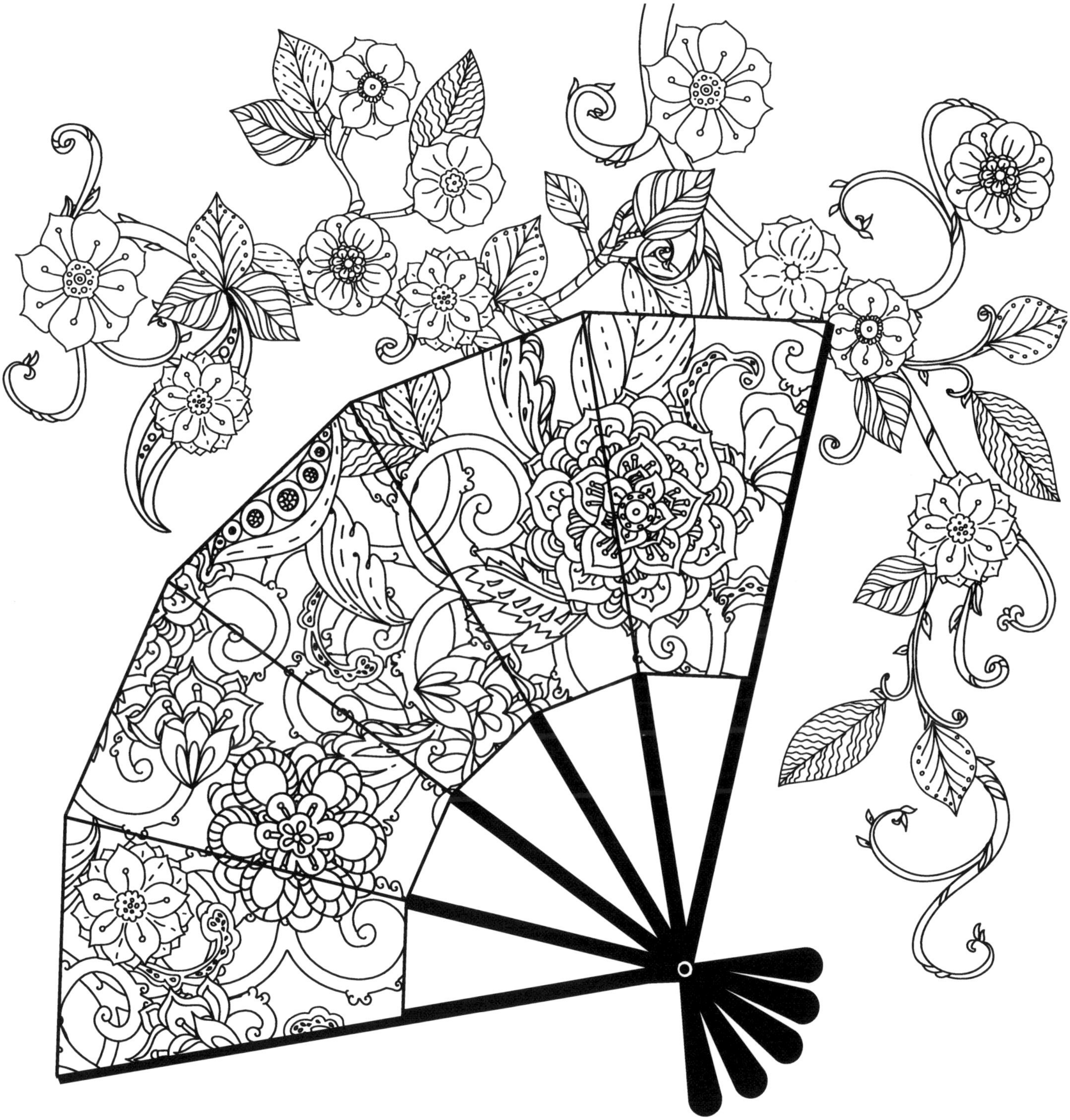

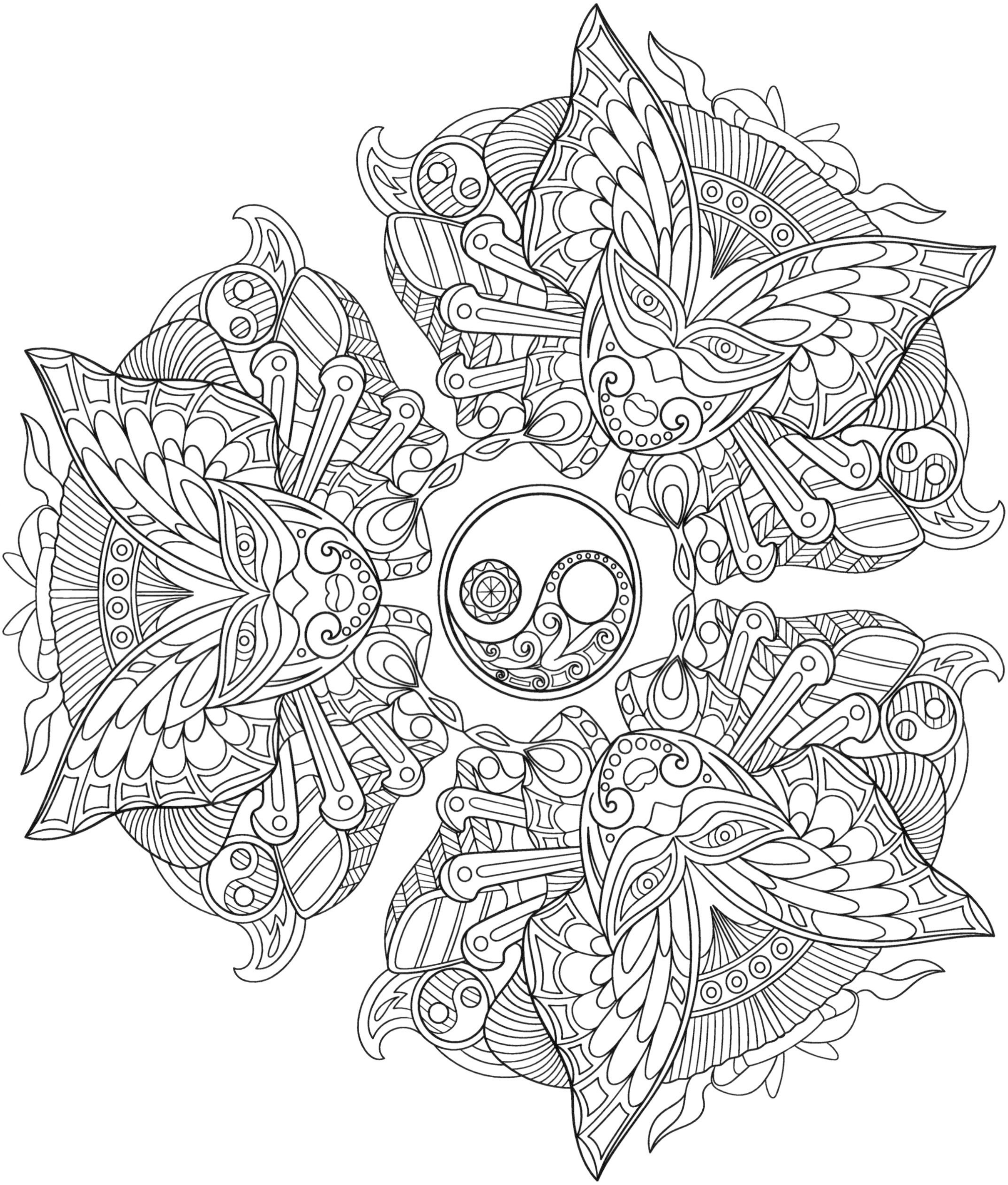

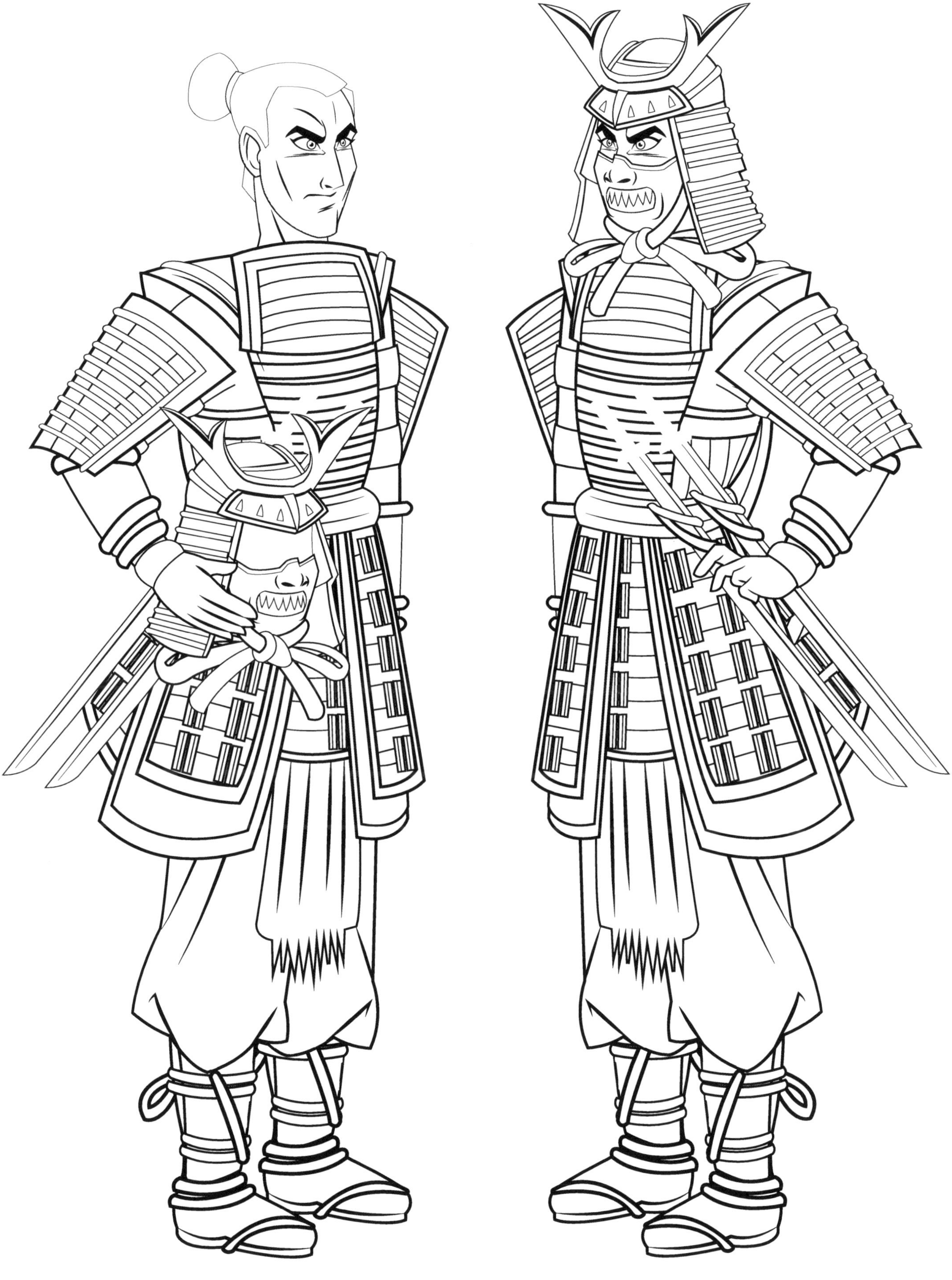

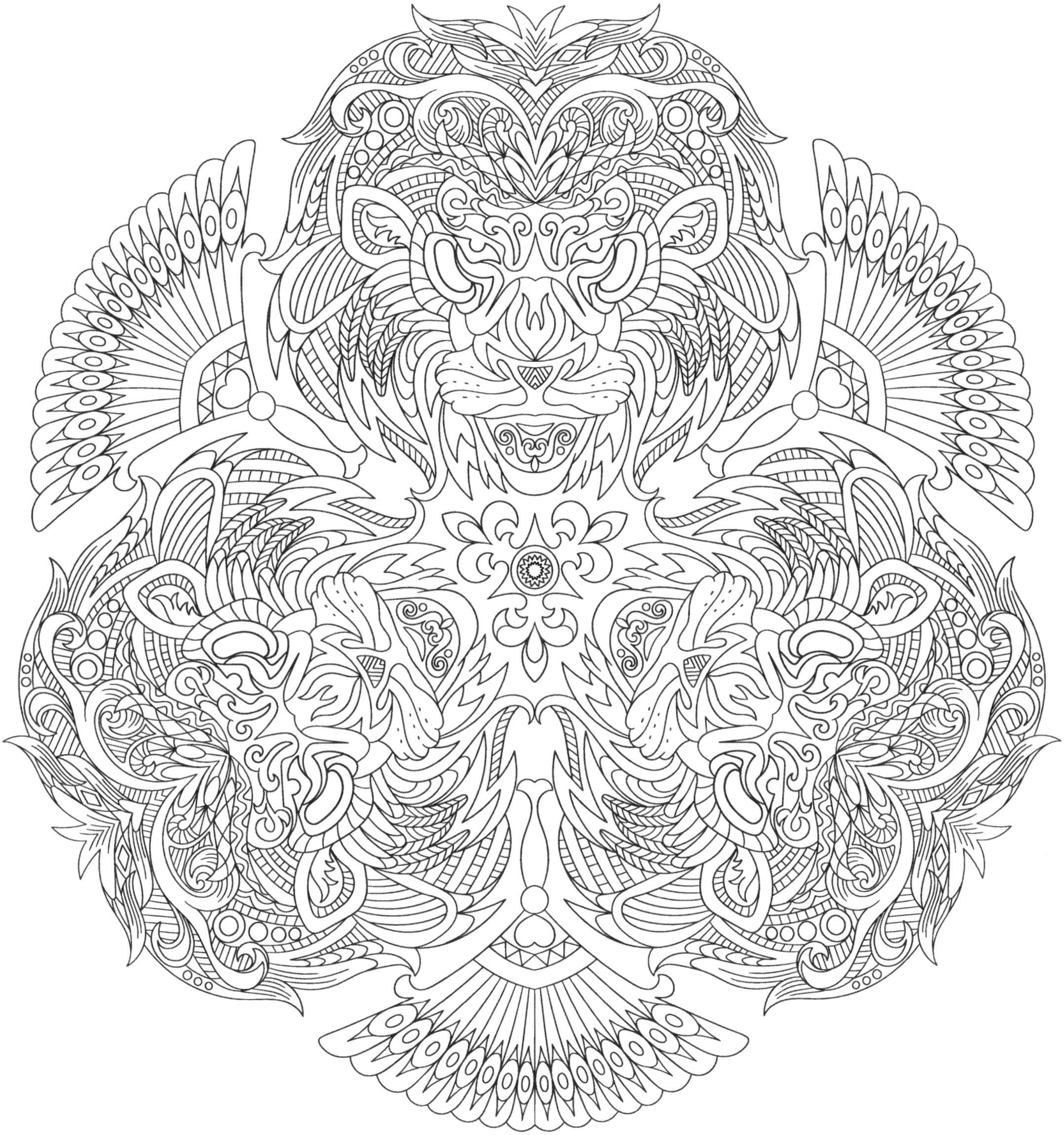

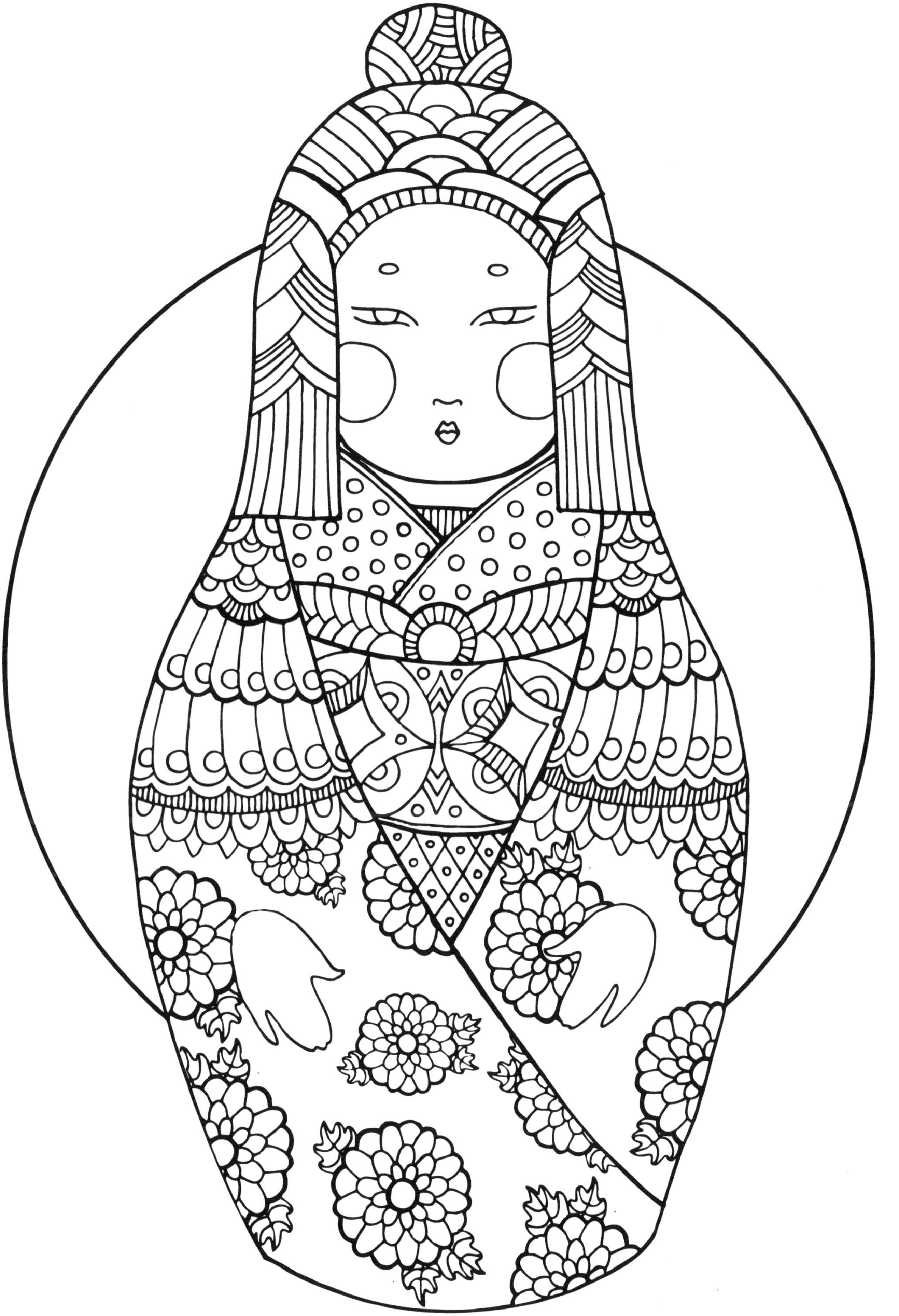

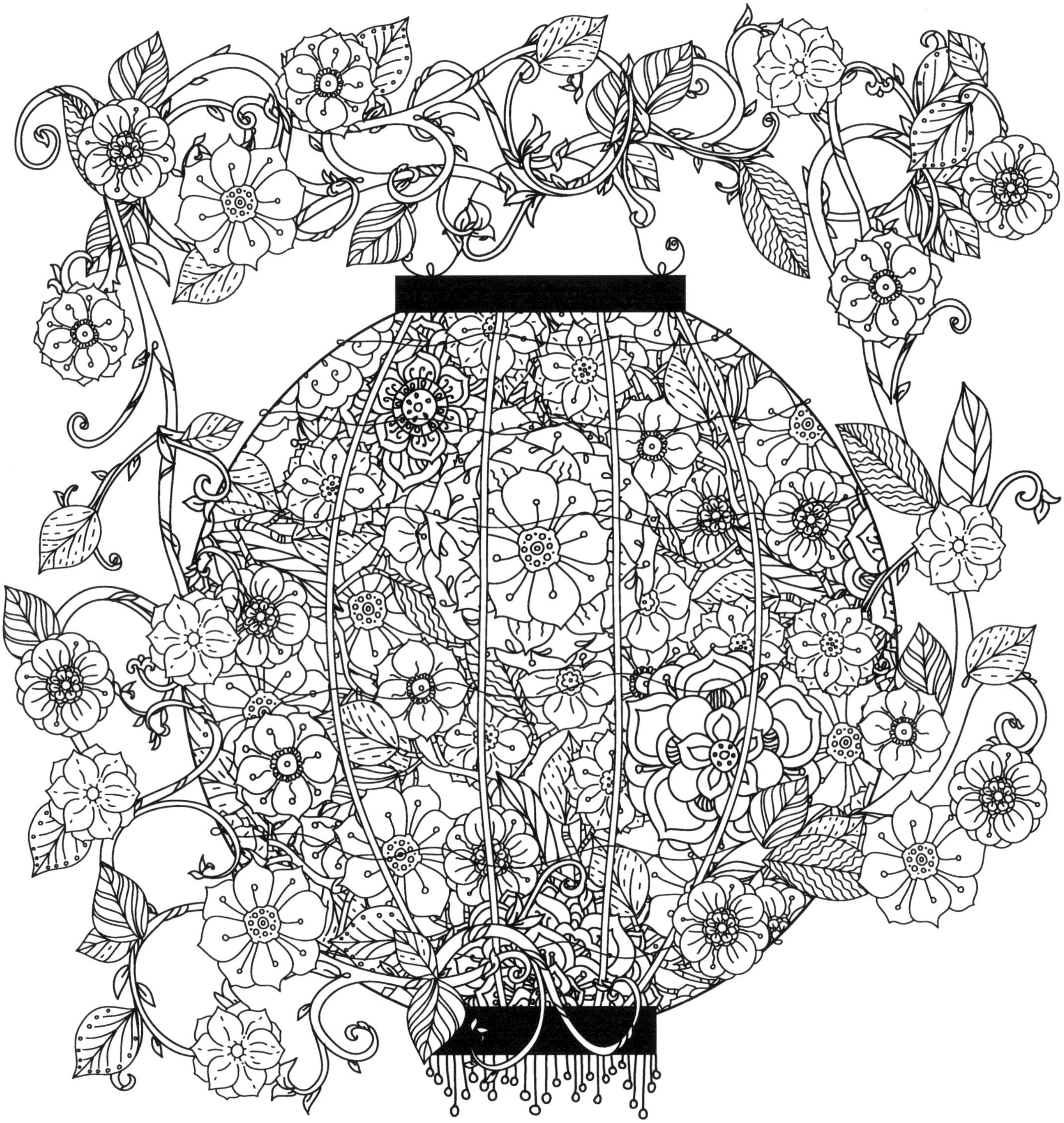

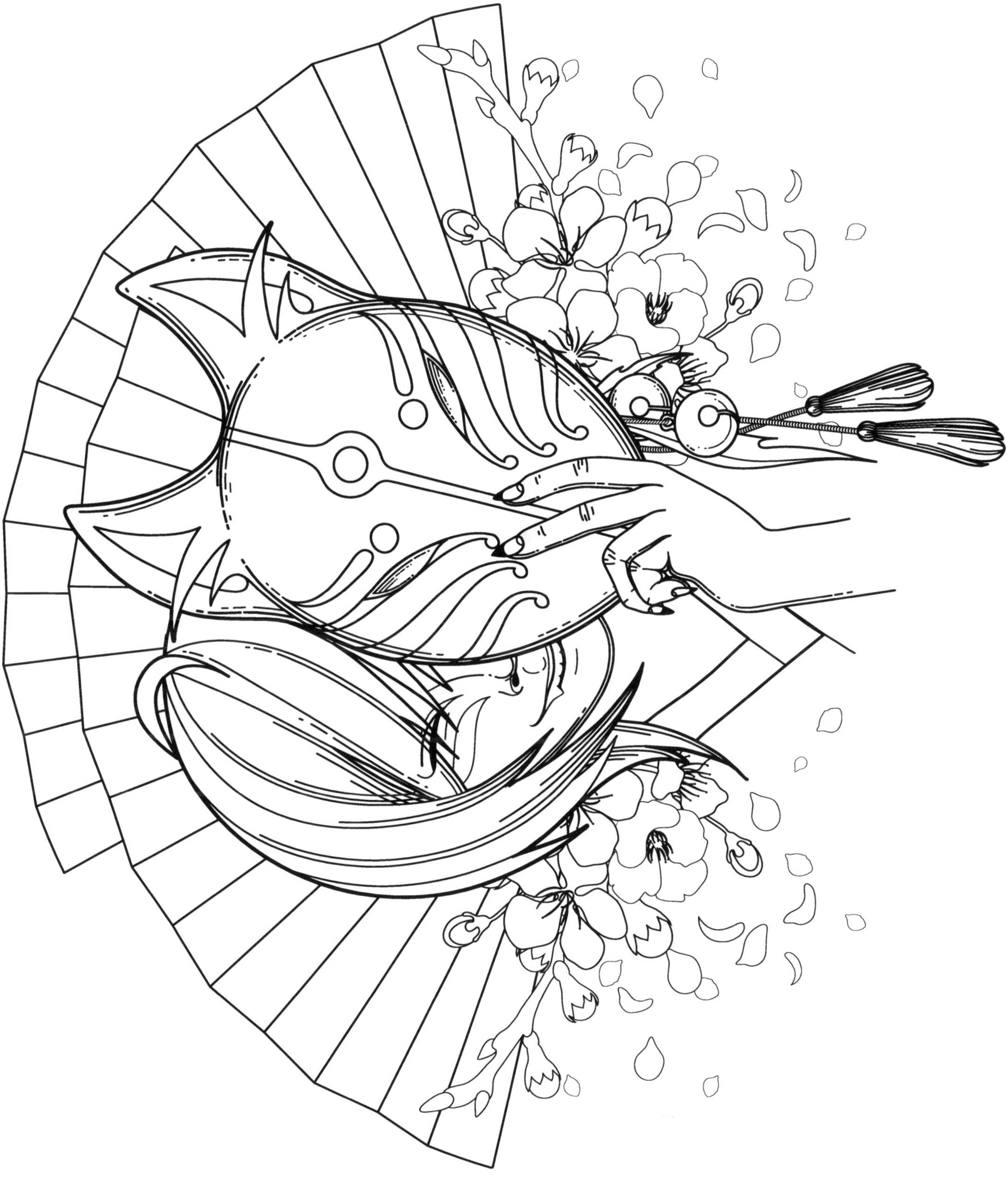

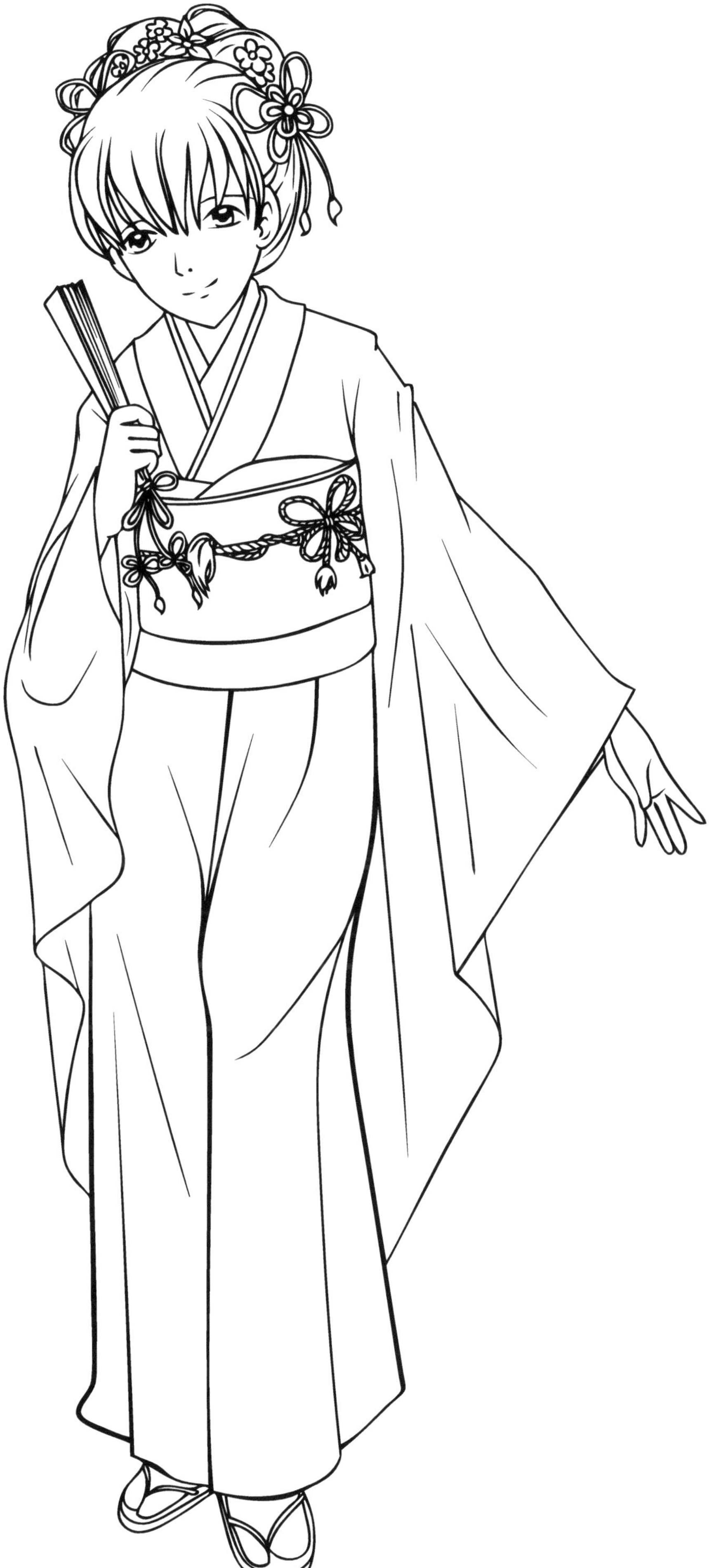

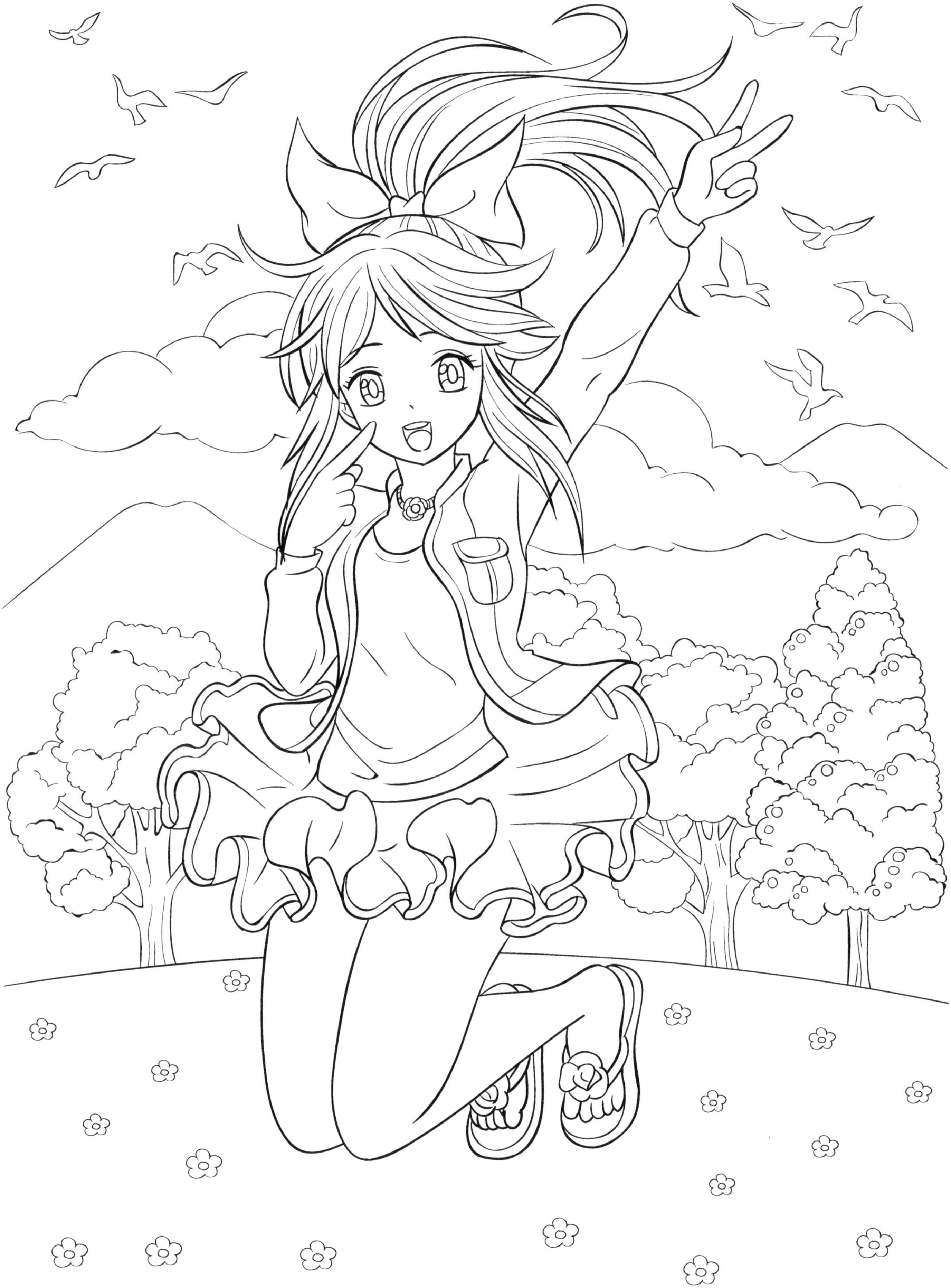

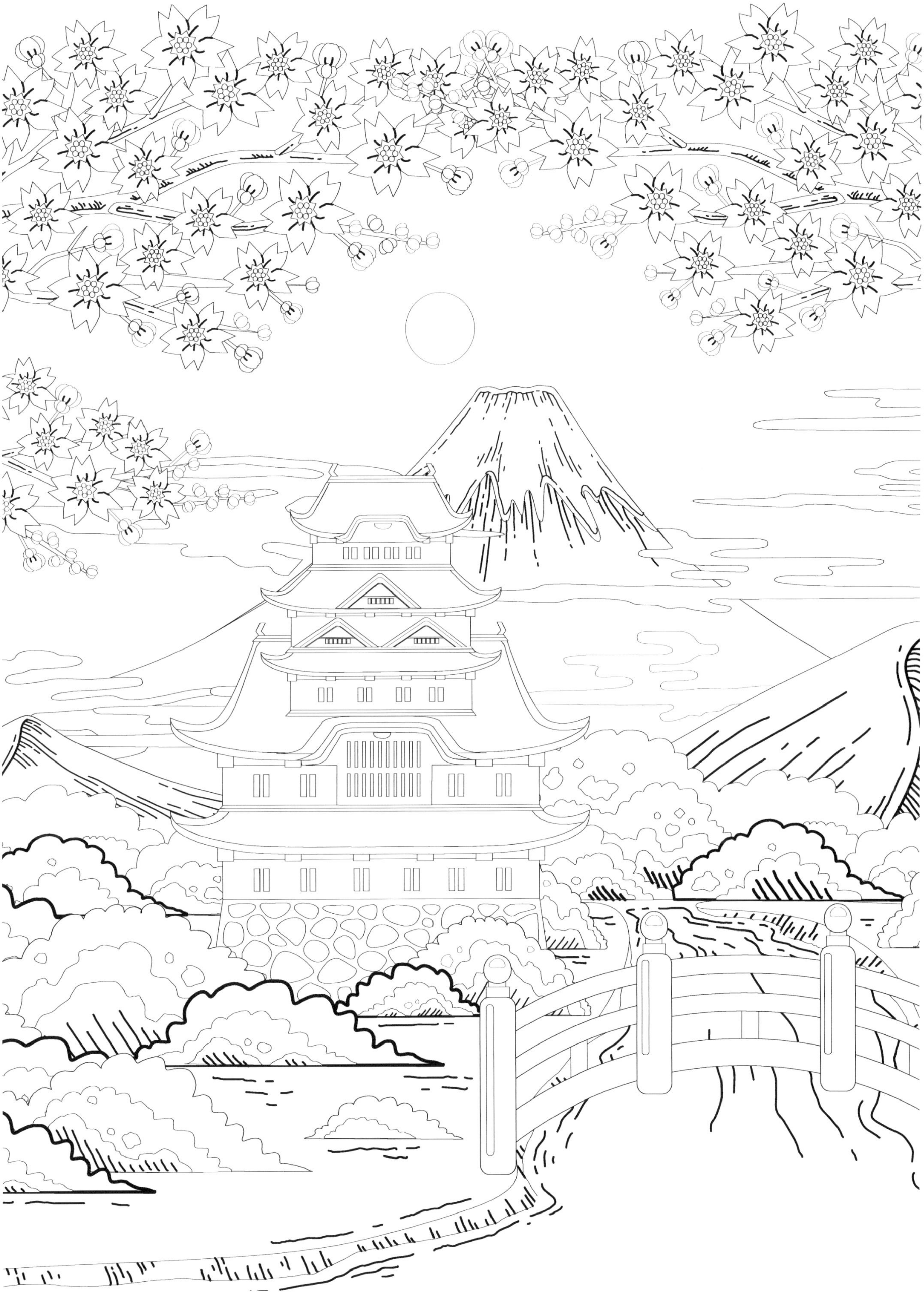

28029120R00035

Printed in Great Britain
by Amazon